THOUGHT FREE GOLF

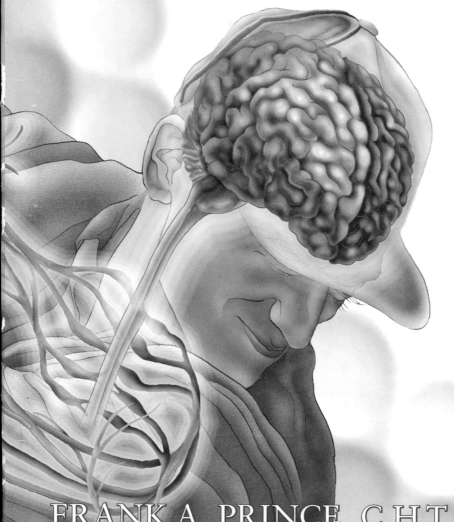

FRANK A. PRINCE, C.H.T.

Thought Free Golf®
Copyright ©2007 Unleash Your Mind Products, L.L.C.

First Printing – 2007
Printed in the United States of America

ISBN: 1-893013-07-3

Publisher and Loving Wife
Cherri Prince

Graphic Design
Louise Marshall Graphic Design

Illustrations
Peter Jurek – www.peterjurek.com

Editor
Robin Prince Monroe – www.robinprincemonroe.com

Unleash Your Mind Products
www.thoughtfreegolf.com
www.speedsleep.com

thought free golf

HOW TO BRING YOUR BEST DRIVING RANGE SWING TO THE FIRST TEE (AND THE REST OF YOUR GAME)

BY FRANK A. PRINCE, C.H.T.

FOREWORD

As the publisher of *Golf Magazine,* I've seen hundreds of products that claim improvements to your golf game. I was intrigued by *Thought Free Golf* when Frank first introduced it to me because it uses some powerful mental techniques I know work. I had previously worked with Frank to develop high performance skills with my team here at *Golf Magazine*. In the process, Frank demonstrated the power of the subconscious mind by putting my team to deep sleep in minutes. They got a full night's sleep in about half an hour. It was incredible.

Some of the great golfers like Fred Couples have been asked, "What are you thinking when you swing?" And, in true Fred fashion he says, "absolutely nothing!" Now, I'm a lot like other golfers and it seems almost impossible not to think, analyze and ponder before every swing. Mastering the skill of thinking "absolutely nothing" is exactly what *Thought Free Golf* delivers. What makes *Thought Free Golf* different is that it's not a product that focuses on your stance or your grip or any of your swing mechanics. It provides a mental thought routine for the first tee to the last tee and any swing in between.

Most golfers acknowledge the importance of the mental side of the game, but very few practice these skills. Most just don't know how. I appreciate how Frank boiled it down into some simple principles and an easy process to follow. It works for me, and I'm sure it will work for you too. It's a no-brainer.

Chris Wightman
Publisher, *Golf Magazine*
September 5, 2006

CONTENTS

THE SWING

YOU WIRED INTO YOUR BRAIN

section 1

Studies in motor learning show that once a skill is learned it is never forgotten. Furthermore, after ten days of retraining, the skill level will return to as much as eighty percent efficiency, even after a year without practice. Like other motor skills such as shoe tying, bike riding, and swimming, your golf swing, once learned, is a motor program that is captured permanently in the neural networks of your brain.

There are, however, circumstances that can deny you full access to that motor program. When this happens you may find that your "A" swing – the one that fires on all cylinders – is temporarily unavailable. It is not uncommon to hear a golfer say, *"I wish I could bring my driving range swing to the first tee."* Even those who have spent the time necessary to develop consistency on the driving range can have difficulty transferring that swing to that first shot and then to the rest of the game.

Most would admit that this problem is mental. Think of all that goes through your mind as you walk to that first tee. You are aware of others playing or watching. You want to get off to a good start and you want your score to be competitive. Back on the driving range there is little concern if you make a bad shot. Your mind is free to let go and allow your body to swing automatically. But on the course, all of a sudden, everything you do is measured. Every swing counts.

You know you can make a good swing because you have done it before. You remember clearly those "sweet" shots, the ones that keep you coming back. They are proof that you can do it. They are the evidence that your "A" swing is already programmed into your brain. All you have to do is find a way to tap into it, and to be able to do it consistently.

PERFORMANCE AFTER RETRAINING
After ten days of retraining, your performance level will return to as much as 80% efficiency.

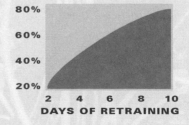

THE CRITICAL
3 MINUTES

section 2

Golfers search endlessly for the perfect swing, but there is a lot more to golf than the swing. Before a tournament pro golfers go through extensive mental as well as physical preparation. They have tools and techniques that prepare both their minds and their bodies. Golf lessons and practice are the ways to prepare your body. *Thought Free Golf* is the way to prepare your mind.

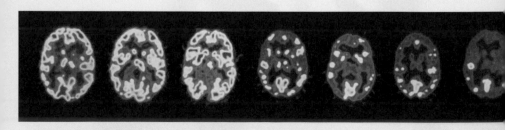

A swing takes approximately two seconds. When you break 90, you swing the club for a total of only **three minutes** out of a four-hour round of golf. Between swings there are long periods of time when your mind can wander. Those three minutes that you are swinging are crucial. To play well your mental state during that time has to be just right. In sports like basketball, soccer or tennis there is very little time to think between shots. Pro athletes say that when they are at their best they are acting and reacting automatically. That acting and reacting without thought is called "flow." They are able to achieve this state of flow because they have taken their physical and mental skills to a high level of unconscious competence.

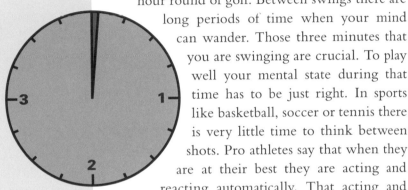

SWING TIME IN A ROUND OF GOLF
3 minutes out of 4 hours

Thought Free Golf makes those three critical minutes a time when your subconscious takes charge and swings for you. It taps into that place in your mind where all your practice has been stored into a skill. It gives you the ability to operate at a level of unconscious competence just like the pros.

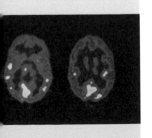

WHAT IS
THOUGHT FREE GOLF?

section 3

SO, WHAT IS *THOUGHT FREE GOLF*?

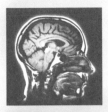

Simply put, *Thought Free Golf* is a mental routine. A routine that allows your mind to become free of conscious thought during your swing. It is a simple 3 step process that allows your body to release your swing without interference from your brain.

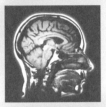

After you develop consistency in your swing mechanics on the driving range, *Thought Free Golf* will help you take that consistency to the course. Once you can swing "thought free" you will have the ability to be on automatic pilot for those few short, crucial seconds that start with your set-up and end in follow through.

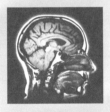

WHAT THOUGHT FREE GOLF IS *NOT*.

Thought Free Golf does not replace skill building. You will still need to master the physical skills required in golf. *Thought Free Golf* is not about altering your swing. But once you have mastered the physical side of the game, it will take you to **the next step – mental mastery.**

THE SECRET

HOW IT WORKS

section 4

Thought Free Golf is about the mastery of your mind during your golf shot. In a golf lesson you learn specific movements that you practice again and again until they become a part of your swing. Ideally, after enough practice, these movements become grooved into your unconscious swing pattern. In that same way, *Thought Free Golf* helps you develop a consistent mental routine so that you can consistently and effortlessly tap into your best practiced swing.

MENTAL MASTERY

We have literally millions of nerve connections in our brain. Recent research shows that with repetitive use these neural pathways can be strengthened. This same research also shows that the pathways we do not use regularly will eventually atrophy like unused muscles. By practicing consistent, repetitive thoughts and actions, we can reinforce these pathways and therefore build skills.

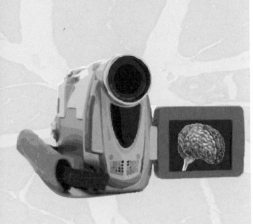

The mind records experience. The brain stores what it sees, hears, and feels into the packets of information that make up memories. The brain can recall experiences so vividly that the body will react as though the experience is concurrent. It doesn't differentiate between something vividly imagined and something real.

To make a mental pathway stronger, all we have to do is replay an experience over and over again. Mental mastery comes when we have practiced a skill in our mind so many times that it becomes part of our neural network. In other words, it becomes hard-wired into our brain.

Through the study of kinesiology, the relationship between anatomy ans movement, we have learned that this kind of mental practice can also help us build muscle memory. When actually performing a skill, our muscles will repeat the pattern that we have practiced mentally.

The *Thought Free Golf* CD is designed to hard-wire the thought routine for your A-swing into your brain. While the driving range provides you with a way to physically practice your shots, *Thought Free Golf* provides a way for you to practice mentally. All you have to do is take the time to listen to the CD. The more you listen, the more you will reinforce the pattern.

The greatest
sound
in golf is
the woosh,
woosh,
woosh
of your
opponent's
club as
he hurls it
across the
fairway.

WHEN THE WHEELS

FALL OFF

Most people who play golf for a while find that eliminating the tensions and distractions that result from thinking during a shot is very difficult. Mental mastery requires us to eliminate distractions during our swing. The things that distract us can be separated into two groups: external and internal.

"I'm hitting the woods just great, but I'm having a terrible time getting out of them."
Rodney Dangerfield

EXTERNAL OR "SENSOR THINK"

Our brains gather information visually, auditorally and kinesthetically. If a fly lands on your golf ball when you are set for a shot, it can distract you. Another golfer's sneeze, a bird's call, or the wind rustling your jacket can also sidetrack you. These external sensory stimulations can grab your train of thought and cause "sensor thinking" to occur. When this happens, your mind is diverted from your swing to the distraction. It focuses on what it is seeing, hearing, or feeling and reacts to the stimulus. Having mental mastery means being able to block out this kind of external stimuli. It is the ability to shut out all external distractions at specific, critical moments and it is the first right of passage into the world of a pro.

THE BRAIN:

Your brain makes sensory predictions. The neurons in your brain become active even before they receive sensory input. They actually anticipate what you might see, hear or feel at any given moment. Confidence results from a pattern of correct neurological predictions. The *Thought Free Golf* process is designed to establish a pattern in your brain that will then give you confidence in your swing.

INTERNAL OR "TINKER THINK"

You can become distracted internally when you force your mind to focus on things you want to happen. When you try to "tweak" your swing in order to improve it, you think through each move – sometimes even talking to yourself during your swing – believing this "tinker thinking" may help. The truth is, this technical coaching from within shifts focus away from your natural, practiced swing. You don't tolerate others distracting you, yet internally you allow your own "inner voice" to do the very same thing. The urge to "tinker think" is strong, yet the reality is that in the few moments it takes to complete your swing, there's not enough time for the subconscious to internalize then implement these conscious instructions.

The golf swing is a complicated combination of muscular actions which are too complex to be controlled by conscious mental effort. Amazingly, your muscles can get the job done better without conscious thought by relying on unconscious competence or muscle memory. "Tinker thinking" interferes with the muscle memory you have carefully built into your practiced swing. In "tinker thinking" you believe that by making a careful swing you can guide the shot to the place you want it to go. But this carefulness interferes with your free, full swing, and often produces a poor shot.

Being careful equals choke!

HOW THE UNCONSCIOUS CREATES THE
PERFECT SHOT

section 6

When we do let go and allow our body to swing without conscious thought, we draw up the competence stored in our unconscious. The complex muscle and mind activities that become "mastered" require zero conscious thought. You experience this kind of mastery when you ride a bike or drive a car. Have you ever driven home and when you arrived you didn't remember part of the drive? Your conscious mind was thinking of something else while your subconscious drove.

To get good at golf you have to practice. The practice is recorded in muscle memory allowing you to develop an unconscious competence. The whole idea of practice is to record into your memory a good swing. That's the reason golf lessons, and the coaching and feedback that accompany them, are so important.

What some golfers don't realize is that another way to practice is to visualize. You can improve your swing by practicing it in your mind. If you imagine a great swing your subconscious can actually record that pictured experience and then apply it to your physical swing.

Once you have developed a good swing – through coaching, feedback, practice, and visualization – you need is the confidence that your subconscious can call up your "A" swing the course consistently.

When golf courses are designed, the tees are positioned with psychological elements in mind. These psychological challenges can distract you and cause uncertainty. This uncertainty can prevent you from letting go enough for your best swing to be released through your "auto pilot." This is the reason golfers can hit well on the driving range but often struggle on the first tee.

5%

95%

COGNITIVE ACTIVITY
Only 5% of our cognitive activity is in conscious awareness.

According to neuroscientists, we are aware of about five percent of our cognitive activity. Thus, 95% of our brain actually goes beyond our consciousness. We utilize a bit of that 95% when we use a thing called the "adaptive unconscious." The "adaptive unconscious" allows us to do things with high levels of complexity without having to think through every step. An example might be turning a car around a corner without having to go through the calculations to determine the precise angle of the turn, steering radius speed, and velocity of the automobile. Once your "adaptive unconscious" learns the golf swing it can reproduce it with extreme accuracy, as long as you don't interfere with it consciously.

DEVELOPING A CONSISTENT
SWING

section 7

Many people say golf is ninety percent mental and ten percent physical. Well, on the practice range, it needs to be ninety percent physical and ten percent mental.

REPETITION = MUSCLE MEMORY = CONSISTENT SWING

On the driving range, there are 40-50 balls in a bucket. A scratch golfer can complete an entire 18 holes with that many swings – minus his putts of course! How often have you arrived at the course without time to hit the driving range? Pros consistently put time in on the range so they can practice enough to embed their best swing into muscle memory.

Imagine a machine that tests clubs and golf balls. Without thought it delivers a consistent swing based on its set-up. You can deliver a consistent swing based on your set-up, too — if you don't try to adjust mentally during the process. Golf is a game of consistency. You want to be able to swing like that machine.

FIRE TOGETHER – WIRE TOGETHER

In the brain, when two neurons fire at the same time they become stronger. In your golf swing these strengthened neurons are grouped into patterns. They become "wired together". When you use a consistent thought routine with your swing you wire together the physical and mental processes, thus creating the ability to swing without conscious thought.

YOUR
PRE-SHOT
ROUTINE

section 8

Over time a pro golfer develops a consistent pre-shot routine. The goal of the pre-shot routine is to get set-up for the shot. The routine varies from individual to individual, but there are a few things that can help make this routine consistent.

EXAMPLE PRE-SHOT ROUTINE:

Behind the Ball

By the time you are standing behind the ball, you have already selected a club for the shot and have pictured in your mind exactly where you want the ball to go. Stand about five steps behind the ball then stop to focus.

Next, take your stance and make a few practice swings. This gives your body a positive frame of reference, readying it for the *Thought Free Golf* shot.

Walk up to the Ball

As you walk up to the ball, keep the target in the center of your vision. By doing this you create a strong visual memory in your brain. Sports like basketball and baseball allow the athlete to keep the target in their field of vision, but the very nature of golf requires a turning away. Golfers are forced to take a blind shot. Fortunately, humans have strong visual memory, so even though we can't keep our eyes on the target, we can rely on our "mind's eye" to function in a similar way.

Stand Over the Ball

Once you arrive at the ball, align your feet. A horizontal line across the tips of your toes should point towards the target. Take a look at your target one last time to make sure you are correctly aligned. Look back at the ball. **Now, you are ready.** You have completed your pre-shot routine.

It is at this point that you will begin your *Thought Free Golf* routine, by saying to yourself **"READY."**

The key to using a pre-shot routine is consistency. It is important to use this routine every time you take a shot. This consistent pre-shot routine will enable you to feel confident when you say **"READY."** The word **"READY"** will be the first signal to your brain that you are about to take a *Thought Free Golf* swing.

YOUR

THOUGHT

ROUTINE

section 9

Most golfers have a swing routine, but few have a "thought" routine. A swing routine provides a consistent set-up for a shot. A thought routine provides a consistent swing. *Thought Free Golf* is achieved by developing a simple thought routine.

The thought routine can be broken down into three points: between shot thoughts, set-up thoughts and swing thoughts.

1. BETWEEN SHOT THOUGHTS

The time to create your desired outcome is well before you set-up for a shot. During those moments between swings you are presented with an unlimited number of shot possibilities. The very next swing could produce the perfect shot, or it could land your ball in a bird's nest. It is easy to find yourself thinking about what might go wrong or what you don't want to do. And negative thoughts more often than not produce negative results. So, instead of trying to avoid making a mistake, focus your mind on your desired outcome. Know your goal, and visualize yourself achieving it. Being positive during this time between swings will not only help you make a better shot, it will also help you enjoy the game. The time on the course is for many golfers the best part of their week. Remember, this is supposed to be fun!

2. SET-UP THOUGHTS

Set-up thoughts begin with your swing routine and conclude when you can say to yourself, with conviction, that you are ready to swing. The goal of this mental set-up is to bring you to a cool confidence, a firm knowledge that you are ready to make your best shot. *Thought Free Golf* prepares your mind by aligning your set-up thoughts with your swing routine. With mind and body in sync, all that is left for you to do is relax and make your swing.

3. SWING THOUGHTS

The best swing thoughts are no thoughts. *Thought Free Golf* enables your subconscious to take over so you can create the best outcome for your shot. The goal is for your mind to go blank for those few short seconds during the swing so that your next conscious thought comes after the follow through when you are watching the ball travel toward the green. It is this perfect skip in time that allows you to swing without interference. You can simply let go and swing "thought free."

HOW TO DO IT!

section 10

THE *THOUGHT FREE GOLF* PROCESS

To become consistently "thought free" during your swing, you will simply repeat the following three steps on every shot:

READY
RELAX
RELEASE

These steps will become the triggers that allow your conscious mind to shut down so you can swing "thought free." But in order for it to work each step needs to be "anchored" in your subconscious. By repeatedly listening to the *Thought Free Golf* CD you can anchor these triggers in your mind and establish an unconscious response to each word.

READY
RELAX
RELEASE

STEP 1: READY

Every golfer has had the experience of preparing for a shot and not feeling comfortable with some aspect of the set-up. If you "go ahead and hit it anyway," you usually end up with a bad result. The "ready" step will bring you to a point of comfort and confidence.

When you have finished your swing routine, and you are set with your club behind the ball, you will say the word, **"Ready"** to yourself. When you hear **"Ready"** you will automatically feel confident because, through the use of the *Thought Free Golf* CD, you have trained your mind to respond the minute you set your body. When you say to yourself, **"Ready"** you will feel comfortable and ready to make your best shot. If for some reason you find yourself distracted or uneasy, take the time to set your mind again. When you can say to yourself, **"Ready"** with confidence, you are set. Now move on to the next step.

STEP 2: RELAX

In golf, one of the most common causes of error is over-tightening. This is apparent when a golfer exerts a lot of effort to produce the power to "hit the ball hard." Practice hard-wires your brain with the balance between relaxing and contracting your muscles that is required for a good shot. You can tap into this balance by allowing your body to relax and be controlled by your subconscious.

One method to get yourself into the balanced, relaxed state that is required to hit the ball well is to tighten your muscles and then let them go. This action will reset your muscles so that they can respond more readily to your subconscious.

Take a moment sometime to notice how relaxed you feel after you sigh. Our bodies have been programmed to relax automatically when we take a slow, deep breath. And taking a deep breath has the added benefit of providing the muscle cells with a fresh supply of oxygen, making them ready to do their best work.

Deep abdominal breathing
is relaxing because it increases
the efficiency of taking in oxygen
and expelling carbon dioxide.

So, in **Step 2: Relax,** you first take a deep breath, then tighten your muscles a few at a time beginning with your legs, then going on up through your trunk, then down your arms, to your hands, and finally all the way to your club. When you feel the grip on your club tighten, you slowly let your breath out, relaxing all of your muscles while saying the word, **"Relax."** This word will trigger your body to release the undesired tension allowing you to make a balanced swing. The *Thought Free Golf* CD trains your mind and body to quickly release unwanted tension when you say to yourself **"Relax."** This relaxation process will also slow down your conscious mind in preparation for the next step.

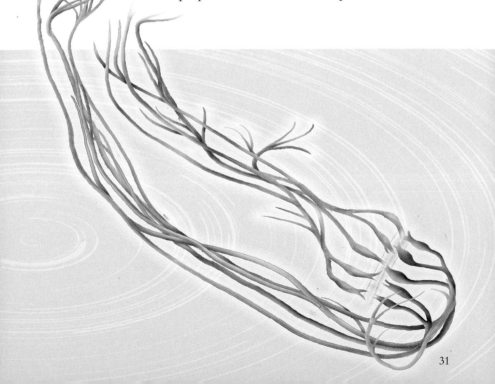

READY
RELAX
RELEASE

STEP 3: RELEASE

When you've gotten your mind and body **Ready** and **Relaxed,** it is time to swing. The word, **"Release"** will be your mind's signal to let go of all thought and body control so that your subconscious can take over and make the swing from muscle memory.

Once you complete the **"Ready"** and **"Relax"** steps, you will say to yourself, **"Release,"** and you will swing. By listening to the *Thought Free Golf* CD, you have trained your brain to release conscious thoughts and control when you use this trigger word. This allows your conscious mind to shut down so you can make a truly "thought free" swing. Your conscious mind will regain focused awareness at the end of the swing as you watch the ball traveling toward your desired goal. Watch the ball until it stops. Then take a moment to appreciate how it felt, and to enjoy the results.

These three steps will enable you to develop a thought routine that will help you carry your driving range swing to the course. The words **Ready, Relax,** and **Release** are the triggers that will guide your mind from conscious awareness to subconscious competence.

The *Thought Free Golf* CD is designed to embed this routine into your subconscious. Listening to it again and again is a way to practice your thought routine. With enough repetition, you will find you will begin to perform it the same way you perform routine daily tasks such as walking and breathing – naturally and without conscious thought.

UNCONSCIOUS
COMPETENCE

section 11

To build competence
in a task, we go through
four stages of learning:

Stage 1: Unconscious Incompetence

Stage 2: Conscious Incompetence

Stage 3: Conscious Competence

Stage 4: Unconscious Competence

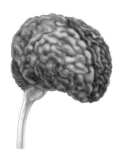

STAGE 1: UNCONSCIOUS INCOMPETENCE

This phase of learning is called the "Ignorance is Bliss" stage. It is that time when you are just starting out, and you really don't know what you don't know. You haven't mastered the skills of the game (incompetence) and you are unaware of exactly what needs to be mastered (unconscious). Increasing your awareness of how the brain affects your swing is the key to moving beyond this first step.

STAGE 2: CONSCIOUS INCOMPETENCE

At this point, you are aware, sometimes painfully, of your lack of a specific skill or knowledge of some points of the game. As you practice becoming "thought free" you may begin to see that you need more "swing mechanics" practice. This stage of learning is by far the most frustrating. It is at this point that you must assure yourself that it *can* be done and that *you* can do it! Moving beyond this step requires you to dissect each skill into incremental parts then practice them.

STAGE 3: CONSCIOUS COMPETENCE

The Conscious Competence stage demands extreme concentration. During this phase you have to think through each and every step, trying not to miss one. At this point your swing is very mechanical and does not fit that pre-course vision of the effortless, perfect swing. Thinking too hard about your swing often results in making a mechanical, segmented swing rather than the smooth, follow-through swing that will consistently produce the best shots. You may come off the course feeling overly tired, due to the extended period of intense concentration (or apprehension) you have just experienced. This is where the dedicated practice of the **Ready, Relax,** and **Release** process will really begin to pay off. Moving beyond this stage requires the discipline of practicing your thought routine with consistency. This is the place where you begin to hard-wire your brain to make the perfect swing the same way you have hard-wired your body.

"Golf is like acting. It takes a lot of focus and preparation, so that you don't have to think about what you're going to do, but can react. Having enough skill and training to react naturally, and not worry about anything else, so that the character you are playing is second-nature, is the key."
Samuel L. Jackson

STAGE 4: UNCONSCIOUS COMPETENCE

At this stage, an observer would consider you to be a "natural." Everything is effortless. Mastery of skills is at the point where flawless execution is second nature and not consciously analyzed. Reactions become virtually instinctive. But even the pros who have reached this stage will occasionally experience a situation like skulling the ball or driving it deep into the woods.

The skill level of unconscious competence is difficult to attain, and even more difficult to maintain. It is the result of moving through the three previous stages and hard-wiring the skills (attainment) as well as the continual execution of those skills through practice (maintenance). *Thought Free Golf* is one tool that can help you gain then maintain this level of mastery.

The stage-dependent learning process represents a continuum of skill building and is transferable to a variety of learning situations. It is essential for you to realize that in mastering golf, you are engaged in a process in which there is no finish line. Recognize that you will go though all of these stages, but the rate of which they progress will vary. You may even find yourself in different stages of this process with different parts of your golf game. The goal is for you to continue to improve without forgetting to enjoy the process.

THINKING

BETWEEN SHOTS

section 12

Thought Free Golf focuses on being thought free during your swing. So, what about the rest of the time?

The first step of *Thought Free Golf* requires you to be able to confidently say to yourself **"Ready."** Have you ever played with someone who pulls out an old ball on the tee of a par 3 over water? So much for their confidence! They already believe that they will miss the shot. This kind of low-confidence thinking can happen at any time between swings. Perhaps you see a shot that looks difficult, you feel pressured by others, or you just want to make a great shot so badly that you are pressuring yourself. Your between shot thoughts should reinforce your confidence, not erode it. It is important to focus on what you can do; not what you can't.

When you are on the course as you move to the next hole pay attention to the language you are using with yourself. Your subconscious is paying

Golf
is the
only sport
where
the most
feared
opponent
is you.

close attention to what you are thinking. Have you ever heard someone say "I can't hit a drive" or "I'm not a good putter"? If you tell yourself that long enough, you will find it to be true. Negative language breaks down your confidence; don't bring it out to the course.

To make great shots you need to have the belief that you can. By changing the way you talk to yourself you can plant that belief firmly in your subconscious. So, when you are thinking through your game or talking to your golf buddies, change your language to things like: "I'm getting better at putting!" or "I'm getting to where I can crush it with my driver!".

Remember, at this point, you should have the mechanical skills to hit a great shot with every club in your bag. If not, then you need to go back to the range and practice or sign up for a few more lessons. *Thought Free Golf* comes in when you know how to hit the shots but are having a hard time hitting them consistently.

PRE-GAME

ROUTINE

section 13

Another part of golf that has a significant impact on your mental game is your pre-game routine.

How many times have you seen a player park his car, grab his bag, sign in, then rush to the first tee without any warm-up? This kind of hurrying is typical for many players. A pre-game routine is critical because it prepares your mind and body to function their best.

Just like your body needs a stretch and a warm-up, your mind needs a routine that will allow you to relax on your very first swing. You will have to figure out the pre-game routine that works best for you, but the following is an example of a pre-game routine that prepares the body and focuses the mind:

1. GET TO THE COURSE 45 MINUTES BEFORE YOUR TEE TIME.

Simply getting to the course early enough so you don't have to rush around will improve your mindset. Not only will this extra time allow you to warm up physically, but it will also allow you to calm down mentally.

2. TAKE CARE OF BUSINESS.

Sign in, change shoes, etc. You will find that not having to rush will make everything about the game ahead better.

3. GO TO THE PRACTICE GREEN FIRST.

Putting is a major part of your game. Spend at least 5 minutes there. This will give you a chance to tap into the muscle memory that contains your best stroke motion. It also gives you an opportunity to check how the greens are playing. Are they fast today, slow, hard, soft? Putt a few balls from various distances. Take your time, and have fun! Remember, you arrived there early enough and you've got plenty of time.

The more you practice, the luckier you get.

4. SPEND SOME TIME CHIPPING A FEW BALLS FROM JUST OFF THE PRACTICE GREEN.

This will give you an even better feel for how the ball will roll and also give you a feel for how the fringe is going to act. Hit at least three balls from each side of the green. This warm up session is to help you identify how the ball is going to run once it lands on the green. You will want to pay special attention to the speed. Knowing if the greens are fast or slow will save you on the course. If you don't have time for the full regimen, then at least chip a few balls to get some idea of the green's behavior. The amount of time the chipping warm-up will take depends on the player, but usually about ten minutes will do. At least half of your warm-up time should be spent on and around the green. The number of strokes you will save later makes this an excellent investment of your time.

5. HEAD TO THE DRIVING RANGE THEN TAKE A FEW MINUTES TO STRETCH.

Stretching your muscles to avoid injury is not the same thing as warming-up with pre-game swings. It is important to stretch before you take a full swing with your club.

6. FINALLY, IT'S TIME FOR A FEW PRACTICE SWINGS.

Start with your wedges and remember to make full, smooth swings. After you've hit a few wedge shots, move up to your short irons and, again, hit using a smooth motion. Don't try to be fancy, just get a sense of smoothness and rhythm. That sense of rhythm is something that you will carry to the first tee, so let sink in as you practice. Making these practice shots will also improve your range of motion. This will help a great deal once you get on the course. You'll want to practice with your woods in the same manner. Start with the shortest wood and move up to your driver. Again, make full-motion practice shots and try to get that "centered" feeling.

7. MAKE SURE TO END YOUR PRACTICE IN TIME TO TAKE A CALM WALK TO THE FIRST TEE.

You have spent the time necessary to prepare yourself. Don't let hurrying spoil the work you've done. Walk slowly and calmly to the first tee, taking a few deep breaths as you go. This is a good time to enjoy the beautiful surroundings. Being relaxed and confident when you tee up that first ball will go a long way towards improving your overall game.

MASTERING

THE SKILL

section 14

In summary, in order to incorporate
Thought Free Golf into your game you must
master it as a skill.

In order to build any skill we go through a
series of steps. It is the repetition of these steps
that moves us to mastery of the skill.

The graph represents the steps involved in
skill-building.

LEARNIN

DESIRE

FEEDBACK

PRACTICE/PLAY

LEARNING ACTIVITY

DESIRE

TIME

SKILL-BUILDING STEPS

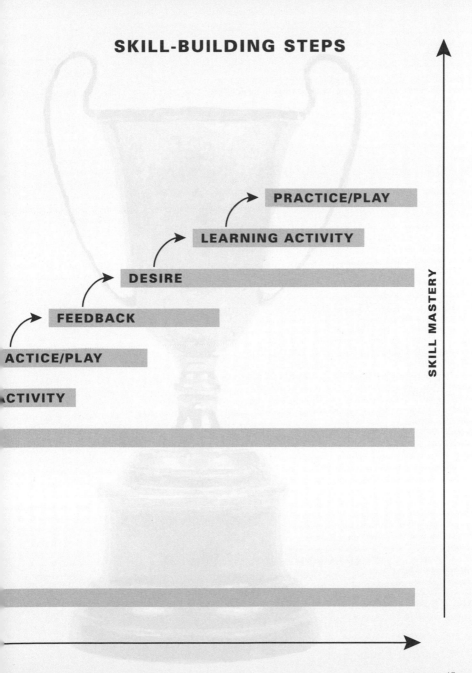

PRACTICE/PLAY

LEARNING ACTIVITY

DESIRE

FEEDBACK

ACTICE/PLAY

CTIVITY

SKILL MASTERY

45

DESIRE TO LEARN

The first step is simply the **DESIRE TO LEARN** a new skill. The stronger the desire, the more driven you are to build the skill.

LEARNING ACTIVITIES

The second step involves experimentation or **LEARNING ACTIVITIES.** Learning activities come in many forms, from formal to very informal. You might actually take a lesson, or you may just jump in and "give it a try" by emulating others. Learning activities give you a mental understanding of the desired skill.

PRACTICE/PLAY

Next, you **PRACTICE.** It is through practice that you "hard-wire" the learning into your mind and body. The more you practice the same action with consistency, the easier it becomes to duplicate. Each time you play, it is practice. Your mind and body learn from each and every shot. With enough practice and playing, you can perform a skill without thinking about it, you become unconsciously competent.

FEEDBACK

For skills to continue to improve, a fourth step is required. This step involves **FEEDBACK.** You can practice and practice, but if you are practicing the wrong way, you may never develop mastery. Feedback provides you with an awareness of how well you are performing. In sports, it can be in the form of a score that measures your ability in numbers. It can also come from a coach who observes you then communicates what he sees.

Feedback often increases your desire to learn, which then circles you back to the first step, **DESIRE.** Then the skill building process is repeated, this time at a higher skill level. Circling through these skill-building steps will eventually create the mastery of a skill.

In each of these steps it is important for you to experience positive results. On a psychological level, human beings move toward pleasure and away from pain. If you are told you MUST learn a skill but you have no DESIRE to learn it, you will never really master the skill and what you do learn will eventually dissipate. If you do not enjoy the **LEARNING ACTIVITY** you will not want to practice, and what little you have learned will dissolve. If you do not experience positive results from your **PRACTICE** you will not practice anymore which again will cause you to eventually forget all you have learned. Lastly, if you do not experience the kind of **FEEDBACK** that makes it easier for you to perform the skill, you will eventually lose the skill.

Having positive experiences as you make the effort to learn a skill will increase your desire to improve. Positive skill-building experiences come in the form of learning activities you enjoy – a perfect shot, and good feedback from a coach, or a competitive score. When your desire to master a skill is strong you become more willing to take the time to educate yourself, practice, and seek feedback so that you can improve.

Now, it is up to you. Take the steps to master the skill of *Thought Free Golf.*

FRANK A. PRINCE, C.H.T.

Frank Prince is President and Founder of Unleash Your Mind Consulting and the author of seven books on creativity and the human mind. He has dedicated his career to helping people shift limiting beliefs from handicaps into desired results using simple, proven, easy-to-follow methods. Frank has proven that the power of the subconscious mind is the biggest untapped resource within individuals.

In addition to being a Master Practitioner of Neuro-Linguistic Programming (NLP), Frank is also a National Guild Certified Sports HypnoTherapist (C.H.T.). He uses hypnotherapy to help individuals and teams achieve peak performance – from helping a team win the Baja 1000 Off-Road Race to dramatically improving sales performance at Time Inc. It was through his work with the publishers of *Golf Magazine* that Frank developed a methodology that could successfully be applied to improving golf scores.

He also helps thousands of individuals achieve better health and wellness with his wildly successful series of *Speed Sleep*® CDs (www.speedsleep.com).

Frank is an executive coach for Fortune 50 CEO's. A dynamic and entertaining speaker, Frank is available to deliver keynotes and group demonstrations on the *Thought Free Golf*® methodology. Contact Frank at: www.unleashyourmind.com

THE NATURAL SLEEP PROCESS

SUDDEN INSIGHT

EEG: K-Complex
(30-35 cycles/sec.)

AWAKE & ALERT

EEG: Rapid Beta Waves
(12-32 cycles/sec.)

Normal time to go all the way down about 90 minutes. Speed Sleep® accelerates this process.

HEAD HITS PILLOW

- Calm wakefulness – if nudged a person will claim to be awake
- Breathing slows, muscles grow limp
- Heart rate slows
- Small drop in body temperature

EEG: Alpha Waves
(8-12 cycles/sec.)

SENSORY "VOID" PHASE

STAGE ONE

- Do not consciously hear constant level noises
- Do not consciously smell subtle smells
- Do not consciously feel slight variations in temperature

EEG: Theta Waves
(6-8 cycles/sec.)

STAGE TWO

- A roller coaster stage with faster and slower brain wave activity
- Spikes of activity to the alpha level
- Stage lasts 10 to 15 minutes

EEG: Theta Waves
(4-8 cycles/sec.)

After the first dream, the brain cycles back up to Stage Two to begin a second descent. We repeat this process all night long.

STAGE THREE

- A deep sleep
- Growth hormone is secreted
- Slower overall brain wave activity
- Stage lasts 5 to 15 minutes

EEG: Delta Waves
(2-4 cycles/sec.)

STAGE FOUR

- The deepest of sleep
- REM (Rapid Eye Movement) occurs
- Dreams occur

- Body cell repair increases
- Stage lasts 30 minutes or so

EEG: Delta Waves
(0.5-2 cycles/sec.)